THE CRAZY TIRED BEETCHES STORY

Crazy Tired Beetches is a small, woman-owned company that publishes unique and fun planners, journals and gifts. We believe that cuss words can make you happy, and we are simply a group of women who enjoy laughing at life.

Our journals, planners and calendars are designed for women to pick up, giggle, and share a laugh with their friends, family and colleagues. We are a little bit snarky, a little bit sassy, and a whole lot of fun!

We may cuss (a TON), but we find sometimes a few strategically placed F-Bombs make the stress and insanity of everyday life laughable, and a heck of a lot more enjoyable!

With that, we hope you find a giggle, belly laugh or just smile at our collection of products. If you do, we would love it if you would leave us a review on Amazon!

We are proudly based in the USA and look forward to continuing taking life not too seriously with you!

Sending love from the CTB Crew!

Part of the "Cuss Words Make Me Happy" Series of Journals, Planners and Books

ISBN: 9781790450244

First Published: 11-28-2018

Shit List

for

_____

Another Tired-Ass Woman

Week of _____

SUNDAY	
MONDAY	
TUESDAY	
WEDNESDAY	
THURSDAY	
FRIDAY	
SATURDAY	

This Week's Shit List

Other Shit to Remember

Week of _____

SUNDAY	
MONDAY	
TUESDAY	
WEDNESDAY	
THURSDAY	
FRIDAY	
SATURDAY	

This Week's Shit List

Other Shit to Remember

Week of _____

SUNDAY	
MONDAY	
TUESDAY	
WEDNESDAY	
THURSDAY	
FRIDAY	
SATURDAY	

This Week's Shit List

Other Shit to Remember

Week of _____

SUNDAY	
MONDAY	
TUESDAY	
WEDNESDAY	
THURSDAY	
FRIDAY	
SATURDAY	

This Week's Shit List

_____

_____

_____

_____

_____

_____

_____

_____

_____

_____

_____

_____

Other Shit to Remember

_____

_____

_____

_____

_____

_____

_____

_____

_____

_____

_____

_____

_____

_____

_____

Week of _____

SUNDAY	
MONDAY	
TUESDAY	
WEDNESDAY	
THURSDAY	
FRIDAY	
SATURDAY	

This Week's Shit List

Other Shit to Remember

Week of _____

SUNDAY	
MONDAY	
TUESDAY	
WEDNESDAY	
THURSDAY	
FRIDAY	
SATURDAY	

This Week's Shit List

Other Shit to Remember

Week of _____

SUNDAY	
MONDAY	
TUESDAY	
WEDNESDAY	
THURSDAY	
FRIDAY	
SATURDAY	

This Week's Shit List

_____
_____
_____
_____
_____
_____
_____
_____
_____
_____
_____

Other Shit to Remember

_____
_____
_____
_____
_____
_____
_____
_____
_____
_____
_____
_____
_____
_____

Week of _____

SUNDAY	
MONDAY	
TUESDAY	
WEDNESDAY	
THURSDAY	
FRIDAY	
SATURDAY	

This Week's Shit List

Other Shit to Remember

Week of _____

SUNDAY	
MONDAY	
TUESDAY	
WEDNESDAY	
THURSDAY	
FRIDAY	
SATURDAY	

This Week's Shit List

Other Shit to Remember

Week of _____

SUNDAY

MONDAY

TUESDAY

WEDNESDAY

THURSDAY

FRIDAY

SATURDAY

This Week's Shit List

_____
_____
_____
_____
_____
_____
_____
_____

Other Shit to Remember

_____
_____
_____
_____
_____
_____
_____
_____
_____
_____
_____

Week of _____

SUNDAY	
MONDAY	
TUESDAY	
WEDNESDAY	
THURSDAY	
FRIDAY	
SATURDAY	

This Week's Shit List

_____
_____
_____
_____
_____
_____
_____
_____

Other Shit to Remember

_____
_____
_____
_____
_____
_____
_____
_____
_____
_____
_____
_____
_____

Week of _____

SUNDAY	
MONDAY	
TUESDAY	
WEDNESDAY	
THURSDAY	
FRIDAY	
SATURDAY	

This Week's Shit List

Other Shit to Remember

SUNDAY	
MONDAY	
TUESDAY	
WEDNESDAY	
THURSDAY	
FRIDAY	
SATURDAY	

This Week's Shit List

Other Shit to Remember

Week of _____

SUNDAY	
MONDAY	
TUESDAY	
WEDNESDAY	
THURSDAY	
FRIDAY	
SATURDAY	

This Week's Shit List

Other Shit to Remember

Week of _____

SUNDAY	
MONDAY	
TUESDAY	
WEDNESDAY	
THURSDAY	
FRIDAY	
SATURDAY	

This Week's Shit List

Other Shit to Remember

Week of _____

SUNDAY	
MONDAY	
TUESDAY	
WEDNESDAY	
THURSDAY	
FRIDAY	
SATURDAY	

This Week's Shit List

Other Shit to Remember

Week of _____

SUNDAY

MONDAY

TUESDAY

WEDNESDAY

THURSDAY

FRIDAY

SATURDAY

This Week's Shit List

Other Shit to Remember

Week of _____

SUNDAY	
MONDAY	
TUESDAY	
WEDNESDAY	
THURSDAY	
FRIDAY	
SATURDAY	

This Week's Shit List

Other Shit to Remember

Week of _____

SUNDAY	
MONDAY	
TUESDAY	
WEDNESDAY	
THURSDAY	
FRIDAY	
SATURDAY	

This Week's Shit List

_____
_____
_____
_____
_____
_____
_____
_____
_____

Other Shit to Remember

_____
_____
_____
_____
_____
_____
_____
_____
_____
_____
_____
_____
_____

Week of _____

SUNDAY	
MONDAY	
TUESDAY	
WEDNESDAY	
THURSDAY	
FRIDAY	
SATURDAY	

This Week's Shit List

Other Shit to Remember

Week of _____

SUNDAY	
MONDAY	
TUESDAY	
WEDNESDAY	
THURSDAY	
FRIDAY	
SATURDAY	

This Week's Shit List

Other Shit to Remember

Week of _____

SUNDAY

MONDAY

TUESDAY

WEDNESDAY

THURSDAY

FRIDAY

SATURDAY

This Week's Shit List

_____
_____
_____
_____
_____
_____
_____
_____
_____

Other Shit to Remember

_____
_____
_____
_____
_____
_____
_____
_____
_____
_____
_____
_____
_____

Week of _____

SUNDAY	
MONDAY	
TUESDAY	
WEDNESDAY	
THURSDAY	
FRIDAY	
SATURDAY	

This Week's Shit List

Other Shit to Remember

Week of _____

SUNDAY	
MONDAY	
TUESDAY	
WEDNESDAY	
THURSDAY	
FRIDAY	
SATURDAY	

This Week's Shit List

_____
_____
_____
_____
_____
_____
_____
_____
_____

Other Shit to Remember

_____
_____
_____
_____
_____
_____
_____
_____
_____
_____
_____
_____
_____
_____

Week of _____

SUNDAY	
MONDAY	
TUESDAY	
WEDNESDAY	
THURSDAY	
FRIDAY	
SATURDAY	

This Week's Shit List

_____

_____

_____

_____

_____

_____

_____

_____

_____

Other Shit to Remember

_____

_____

_____

_____

_____

_____

_____

_____

_____

_____

_____

_____

Week of _____

SUNDAY	
MONDAY	
TUESDAY	
WEDNESDAY	
THURSDAY	
FRIDAY	
SATURDAY	

This Week's Shit List

Other Shit to Remember

Week of _____

SUNDAY	
MONDAY	
TUESDAY	
WEDNESDAY	
THURSDAY	
FRIDAY	
SATURDAY	

This Week's Shit List

_____

_____

_____

_____

_____

_____

_____

_____

_____

Other Shit to Remember

_____

_____

_____

_____

_____

_____

_____

_____

_____

_____

_____

_____

_____

Week of _____

SUNDAY	
MONDAY	
TUESDAY	
WEDNESDAY	
THURSDAY	
FRIDAY	
SATURDAY	

This Week's Shit List

_____
_____
_____
_____
_____
_____
_____
_____
_____

Other Shit to Remember

_____
_____
_____
_____
_____
_____
_____
_____
_____
_____
_____
_____

Week of _____

SUNDAY	
MONDAY	
TUESDAY	
WEDNESDAY	
THURSDAY	
FRIDAY	
SATURDAY	

This Week's Shit List

_____
_____
_____
_____
_____
_____
_____
_____

Other Shit to Remember

_____
_____
_____
_____
_____
_____
_____
_____
_____
_____
_____
_____
_____

Week of _____

SUNDAY	
MONDAY	
TUESDAY	
WEDNESDAY	
THURSDAY	
FRIDAY	
SATURDAY	

This Week's Shit List

Other Shit to Remember

Week of _____

SUNDAY	
MONDAY	
TUESDAY	
WEDNESDAY	
THURSDAY	
FRIDAY	
SATURDAY	

This Week's Shit List

Other Shit to Remember

Week of _____

SUNDAY

MONDAY

TUESDAY

WEDNESDAY

THURSDAY

FRIDAY

SATURDAY

This Week's Shit List

Other Shit to Remember

Week of _____

SUNDAY	
MONDAY	
TUESDAY	
WEDNESDAY	
THURSDAY	
FRIDAY	
SATURDAY	

This Week's Shit List

Other Shit to Remember

Week of _____

SUNDAY	
MONDAY	
TUESDAY	
WEDNESDAY	
THURSDAY	
FRIDAY	
SATURDAY	

This Week's Shit List

Other Shit to Remember

Week of _____

SUNDAY	
MONDAY	
TUESDAY	
WEDNESDAY	
THURSDAY	
FRIDAY	
SATURDAY	

This Week's Shit List

Other Shit to Remember

Week of _____

SUNDAY

MONDAY

TUESDAY

WEDNESDAY

THURSDAY

FRIDAY

SATURDAY

This Week's Shit List

Other Shit to Remember

Week of _____

SUNDAY	
MONDAY	
TUESDAY	
WEDNESDAY	
THURSDAY	
FRIDAY	
SATURDAY	

This Week's Shit List

Other Shit to Remember

Week of _____

SUNDAY	
MONDAY	
TUESDAY	
WEDNESDAY	
THURSDAY	
FRIDAY	
SATURDAY	

This Week's Shit List

Other Shit to Remember

Week of _____

SUNDAY

MONDAY

TUESDAY

WEDNESDAY

THURSDAY

FRIDAY

SATURDAY

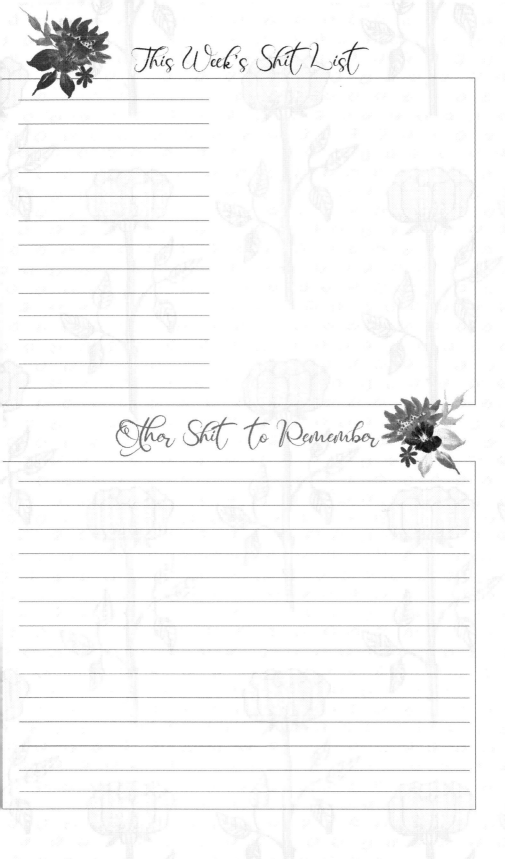

This Week's Shit List

Other Shit to Remember

Week of _____

SUNDAY	
MONDAY	
TUESDAY	
WEDNESDAY	
THURSDAY	
FRIDAY	
SATURDAY	

This Week's Shit List

Other Shit to Remember

Week of _____

SUNDAY	
MONDAY	
TUESDAY	
WEDNESDAY	
THURSDAY	
FRIDAY	
SATURDAY	

This Week's Shit List

Other Shit to Remember

Week of _____

SUNDAY	
MONDAY	
TUESDAY	
WEDNESDAY	
THURSDAY	
FRIDAY	
SATURDAY	

This Week's Shit List

Other Shit to Remember

Week of _____

SUNDAY	
MONDAY	
TUESDAY	
WEDNESDAY	
THURSDAY	
FRIDAY	
SATURDAY	

This Week's Shit List

Other Shit to Remember

Week of _____

SUNDAY	
MONDAY	
TUESDAY	
WEDNESDAY	
THURSDAY	
FRIDAY	
SATURDAY	

This Week's Shit List

_____
_____
_____
_____
_____
_____
_____
_____
_____
_____

Other Shit to Remember

_____
_____
_____
_____
_____
_____
_____
_____
_____
_____
_____
_____
_____
_____

Week of _____

SUNDAY	
MONDAY	
TUESDAY	
WEDNESDAY	
THURSDAY	
FRIDAY	
SATURDAY	

This Week's Shit List

Other Shit to Remember

Week of _____

SUNDAY	
MONDAY	
TUESDAY	
WEDNESDAY	
THURSDAY	
FRIDAY	
SATURDAY	

This Week's Shit List

_____
_____
_____
_____
_____
_____
_____
_____
_____
_____

Other Shit to Remember

_____
_____
_____
_____
_____
_____
_____
_____
_____
_____
_____
_____
_____
_____

Week of _____

SUNDAY	
MONDAY	
TUESDAY	
WEDNESDAY	
THURSDAY	
FRIDAY	
SATURDAY	

This Week's Shit List

Other Shit to Remember

Week of _____

SUNDAY	
MONDAY	
TUESDAY	
WEDNESDAY	
THURSDAY	
FRIDAY	
SATURDAY	

This Week's Shit List

Other Shit to Remember

Week of _____

SUNDAY	
MONDAY	
TUESDAY	
WEDNESDAY	
THURSDAY	
FRIDAY	
SATURDAY	

This Week's Shit List

_____

_____

_____

_____

_____

_____

_____

_____

_____

_____

Other Shit to Remember

_____

_____

_____

_____

_____

_____

_____

_____

_____

_____

_____

_____

_____

_____

SUNDAY

MONDAY

TUESDAY

WEDNESDAY

THURSDAY

FRIDAY

SATURDAY

This Week's Shit List

Other Shit to Remember

Week of _____

SUNDAY	
MONDAY	
TUESDAY	
WEDNESDAY	
THURSDAY	
FRIDAY	
SATURDAY	

This Week's Shit List

Other Shit to Remember

Week of _____

SUNDAY	
MONDAY	
TUESDAY	
WEDNESDAY	
THURSDAY	
FRIDAY	
SATURDAY	

This Week's Shit List

Other Shit to Remember

Week of _____

SUNDAY

MONDAY

TUESDAY

WEDNESDAY

THURSDAY

FRIDAY

SATURDAY

This Week's Shit List

_____
_____
_____
_____
_____
_____
_____
_____
_____
_____

Other Shit to Remember

_____
_____
_____
_____
_____
_____
_____
_____
_____
_____
_____
_____
_____

Week of _____

SUNDAY	
MONDAY	
TUESDAY	
WEDNESDAY	
THURSDAY	
FRIDAY	
SATURDAY	

This Week's Shit List

Other Shit to Remember

Week of _____

SUNDAY	
MONDAY	
TUESDAY	
WEDNESDAY	
THURSDAY	
FRIDAY	
SATURDAY	

This Week's Shit List

Other Shit to Remember

Week of _____

SUNDAY	
MONDAY	
TUESDAY	
WEDNESDAY	
THURSDAY	
FRIDAY	
SATURDAY	

This Week's Shit List

Other Shit to Remember

Week of _____

SUNDAY

MONDAY

TUESDAY

WEDNESDAY

THURSDAY

FRIDAY

SATURDAY

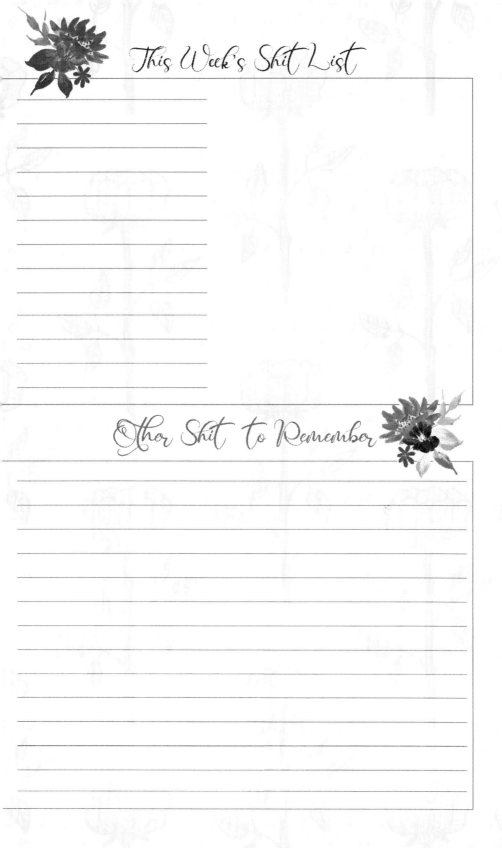

This Week's Shit List

Other Shit to Remember

Week of _____

SUNDAY

MONDAY

TUESDAY

WEDNESDAY

THURSDAY

FRIDAY

SATURDAY

This Week's Shit List

Other Shit to Remember

Week of _____

SUNDAY	
MONDAY	
TUESDAY	
WEDNESDAY	
THURSDAY	
FRIDAY	
SATURDAY	

This Week's Shit List

_____

_____

_____

_____

_____

_____

_____

_____

_____

Other Shit to Remember

_____

_____

_____

_____

_____

_____

_____

_____

_____

_____

_____

Week of _____

SUNDAY

MONDAY

TUESDAY

WEDNESDAY

THURSDAY

FRIDAY

SATURDAY

This Week's Shit List

Other Shit to Remember

Week of _____

SUNDAY	
MONDAY	
TUESDAY	
WEDNESDAY	
THURSDAY	
FRIDAY	
SATURDAY	

This Week's Shit List

Other Shit to Remember

Week of _____

SUNDAY

MONDAY

TUESDAY

WEDNESDAY

THURSDAY

FRIDAY

SATURDAY

This Week's Shit List

Other Shit to Remember

Week of _____

SUNDAY	
MONDAY	
TUESDAY	
WEDNESDAY	
THURSDAY	
FRIDAY	
SATURDAY	

This Week's Shit List

Other Shit to Remember

Week of _____

SUNDAY	
MONDAY	
TUESDAY	
WEDNESDAY	
THURSDAY	
FRIDAY	
SATURDAY	

This Week's Shit List

Other Shit to Remember

Week of _____

SUNDAY	
MONDAY	
TUESDAY	
WEDNESDAY	
THURSDAY	
FRIDAY	
SATURDAY	

This Week's Shit List

Other Shit to Remember

Week of _____

SUNDAY	
MONDAY	
TUESDAY	
WEDNESDAY	
THURSDAY	
FRIDAY	
SATURDAY	

This Week's Shit List

Other Shit to Remember

Week of _____

SUNDAY

MONDAY

TUESDAY

WEDNESDAY

THURSDAY

FRIDAY

SATURDAY

This Week's Shit List

Other Shit to Remember

Week of _____

SUNDAY

MONDAY

TUESDAY

WEDNESDAY

THURSDAY

FRIDAY

SATURDAY

This Week's Shit List

Other Shit to Remember

Week of _____

SUNDAY	
MONDAY	
TUESDAY	
WEDNESDAY	
THURSDAY	
FRIDAY	
SATURDAY	

This Week's Shit List

Other Shit to Remember

Week of _____

SUNDAY	
MONDAY	
TUESDAY	
WEDNESDAY	
THURSDAY	
FRIDAY	
SATURDAY	

This Week's Shit List

Other Shit to Remember

Week of _____

SUNDAY

MONDAY

TUESDAY

WEDNESDAY

THURSDAY

FRIDAY

SATURDAY

This Week's Shit List

Other Shit to Remember

Week of _____

SUNDAY	
MONDAY	
TUESDAY	
WEDNESDAY	
THURSDAY	
FRIDAY	
SATURDAY	

This Week's Shit List

Other Shit to Remember

Week of _____

SUNDAY	
MONDAY	
TUESDAY	
WEDNESDAY	
THURSDAY	
FRIDAY	
SATURDAY	

This Week's Shit List

Other Shit to Remember

Made in United States
Orlando, FL
03 December 2021

11100292R00083